THE 100 BEST
BEDROOMS

BETA-PLUS

THE 100 BEST
BEDROOMS

CONTENTS

THE BEDROOMS OF A HOLIDAY HOME IN RAMATUELLE

Christel De Vos (De Vos Projects) created this newly built villa in
Ramatuelle, in collaboration with Nathalie Mousny.
Christel De Vos also designed all bedrooms in this house.
She found the headboard in an antiques shop. The white painted
Jasno shutters filter out the bright sunlight.

www.devos-interieur.be

RESTORATION OF A 17TH-CENTURY CONVENT FARM

This enclosed convent farm, situated in Flemish Brabant, was built in the seventeenth century with a double wall: one around the farm buildings and one around the farmyard. The low-lying farmhouse was in a very bad state of repair. The house, consisting of two floors and seven bays, the stables and the barn, the gatehouse and the small service buildings were all restored very thoroughly and adapted by architect Bernard De Clerck. Antiques and decoration by Brigitte & Alain Garnier, including for these bedrooms.

info@bernarddeclerck.be   www.garnier.be

ANTIQUES AND CONTEMPORARY ART
IN A MASTER BEDROOM

Antiques dealers Brigitte & Alain Garnier have restored the historic
Vaucelleshof, situated between Bruges and the North Sea coast.
In their master bedroom, they show an exciting blend of contemporary art (Marie-Jo
Lafontaine, Bernar Venet) with exclusive antiques: a rare 18th century Italian console table.

www.garnier.be

AN INTIMATE AND CONTEMPORARY APARTMENT

For this apartment situated in a building from the 1980's belonging to a private domain,
the intervention of Ebony Interiors was requested to create a contemporary universe.
For Ebony, Mario Bruyneel created harmony and comfort using natural and top
quality materials as well as the "Ebony-Interiors Colors" palette of colours.
All the built-in furniture was also designed by him.

www.ebony-interiors.com

The customised bedroom furniture items were realised in natural oak, those of the dressing room in painted MDF in the 'Ebony-Interiors' colours and in leather.

SPACE AND LIGHTNESS IN A VILLA APARTMENT

Gilles de Meulemeester (Ebony Interiors) transformed two ground floor apartments in a building designed by Marc Corbiau into a very large (c. 450 m²) apartment south of Brussels. The master of the house (a loyal customer of Ebony Interiors) asked Gilles de Meulemeester to create a single large, harmonious and warm space. He realised this by revising both the halls, the living rooms and the bedrooms completely. An identical custom-made parquet floor, grey stained oak panelling was installed throughout the entire space. Special attention was paid to the lighting: clear during the day, warm and intimate in the evening.

www.ebony-interiors.com

The guestroom with the custom-made headboard in bleached oak.
Curtains in satin wool.

↖
The master bedroom, with
a custom-made bed in
bleached oak and a padded
leather footstool. Led-
chromed wall lights, silk and
wool bedspread, a carpet
by Jules Flipo (Louisiane
Confort) and an artwork by
Florimond Dufoor.

A CONTEMPORARY SEASIDE VILLA

Interior architect Marie-France Stadsbader transformed these semi-detached houses on the coast into a cosy weekend home for a young family. Despite the limited surface each function was still given its space.

mst@cantillana.com

There is a Cappellini bed in the parents' bedroom and a chair by Hans Wegner and a magnificent Boffi fan as an alternative to air-conditioning in the summer.

The top floor is monochrome white: all the spaces are designed in the same way to form a single whole. White walls combined with a white painted parquet ensure a pleasant living environment.

A HARMONIOUS BLEND

The Dutch interior designer Alexandra Siebelink blends harmoniously pure lines
and a white/beige colour scheme with antique objects in this bedroom.

www.alexandrasiebelink.nl

TRADITIONAL CRAFTSMANSHIP

The doors and window have been made by traditional craftsmanship (Eddy De Prins).
The lighting, the furniture and the mirror have been created by AID Architects.

www.eddydeprins.be   www.aidarchitecten.be

SOBER, SERENE, RELAXING

This bedroom has been designed by interior architect Philip Simoen in his characteristic style: sobere, serene, relaxing, with a preference for warm colours and textures.

www.simoeninterieur.be

The walls have been finished with chalk and varnish.
Chairs by Maxalto (designed by Citterio), plaids by Lenti and Hermès. A Larsen rug and Nogushi lamps. Wooden shutters by Modo.

NATURAL MATERIALS AND PURE LINES

Interior designer Isabelle Bijvoet has created sober lines in this room that is flooded with natural lighting all day. The interior window shutters make it possible to either introduce filtered light or to completely block out the daylight. The laminated cupboard is cleverly inserted into the thickness of the wall thus integrating perfectly into the layout. The plain oak ceiling with a sober palette of colour creates an atmosphere of serenity. All the furniture and accessories in the room were sourced by Isabelle Bijvoet from flea markets.

ib@interd-concept.com

SECULAR PATINA

In this large farm, each room has its own characteristics. Thanks to ancient paint techniques, choice of various antique objects and antique oak floor planks, the bedrooms provide a lived-in timeless atmosphere. A project by Virginie and Odile Dejaegere.

dejaegere_interiors@hotmail.com

THE AMBIENCE OF AN AUTHENTIC SUITE

Themenos has created the ambience of an authentic suite for this villa at the countryside.
The unity of materials and the use of colours emanate a sense of tranquility and space.

www.themenos.be

HOTEL JULIEN

In the historical heart of Antwerp, two houses were restored to form an exceptional accommodation, the Hotel Julien. During the restoration works, all important historical elements have been conserved.

www.hotel-julien.com

A timeless and modern symbiosis of contemporary custom-made elements and furniture design.

↖
Ceiling with exposed beams in original paint texture with painted bark in between the beams.

33

HOST ROOMS IN A SECULAR CASTLE

The history of Chateau de Spycker takes us back to the 12th century. However in 1873, it was completely transformed into a typical French style from the end of the century. The interior is entirely in Napoleon III style.
The Chateau de Spycker has recently undergone a total restoration due to two antique dealer couples who work in the hotel trade. They have taken precaution to preserve the original architectural elements. The castle is presently a place to stay, a private showroom for antiques and exclusive fabrics, and at the same time a place to host privileged guests.

THREE BEDROOMS IN A B&B

With the help of design office Cotwee, the owners of this Bed
& Breakfast in Antwerp have transformed an old building
into an elegant residence of luxury and comfort.
The three host rooms are designed in different colour themes
and come installed with a television and hi-fi set.

The upper storey and stairs of the duplex Dark Room.

The Mocca Rocca Room has a very warm atmosphere.

↖
The White Room inspires
calm, intimacy, simplicity
and purity.

A SANCTUARY OF PEACE

This mansion which dates back to 1884 has had very little work done to it over the years. As a result, the original structures and decorative features have been preserved. However, significant restoration work was required and the techniques used to carry out this work needed to be completely revised. The mansion has a relaxing and timeless feel to it. It has become a home-workshop where Anne Derasse has established her offices; the mansion is a real sanctuary of peace at the heart of the capital.

www.annaderasse.be

Bookcases by Antonio Citterio (Maxalto collection from B&B Italia).
The sofa is also made by Citterio for Maxalto and is covered with wool.
The table in the lounge is by Carlo Colombo (for Zanotta). The table
top is leather and the legs are graphite metal.
The anthracite grey linen wall coverings are lined with light grey silk.
There is a Bram van Velde painting on the chimney breast.

The dressing room has been designed by Anne Derasse; the exterior
has been lacquered in matt MDF. The interior reveals polished oak
ebony; there are identical entrances to the room on either side of the
bed.
Between the headboard and the back of the dressing room there is a
multitude of drawers which open from the side. There is also a Pierre
Alechinsky painting above the bed.

↖
The polished ebony wood creates a sense of intimacy
and the contrast between the anthracite greys and turtle
dove can be found in all the rooms. On the wall, evidence
of the colour charts with threads of silk and wool in the
picture frames.
In the bathroom, a rare Russian marble has been chosen.

A FUSION OF STYLES

This stately country house was built in 1914 and has a living area of 850 m² on a site with a parkland garden of three hectares. During the renovation work, which was managed by Q&M, the style of the house was taken into consideration, but the whole building was brought up to date with cleaner lines and a fusion of styles. The first floor has four bedrooms, two dressing rooms and three bathrooms.

walter.quirynen@skynet.be

Catalini lights create enchanting
illumination in the evening.

The dressing room beside
the bedroom, built by Apart
Keukens. An antique burner
has been retained here as well.

↖
The master bedroom has
wallpaper by Arte. Antique
safety-deposit boxes as
bedside tables.

A STATELY COUNTRY HOUSE

Vlassak-Verhulst, the exclusive villa construction company, built
this stately country house with a number of outbuildings.
The house, situated in magnificent natural surroundings near Bergen aan
Zee (Dutch coast), was then handed over to Sphere Concepts, who assumed
responsibility for the entire design and creation of the interior.

www.sphereconcepts.be

Behind the bed, an illuminated alcove. All of the cupboards have a high-gloss finish.

↖
The handmade Nilson boxspring is built entirely with natural materials. Accent wall in Abysse by Flamant.

A SENSUAL, RELAXING ATMOSPHERE

This bedroom has been created by Hans Verstuyft Architects.
The bedroom corridor has a sensual, relaxing atmosphere: lots of natural
light and contact with a floor in untreated natural stone.

www.hansverstuyftarchitecten.be

SEDUCED BY NATURE AND MINIMALISM

In the green countryside of Antwerp, a couple of decorators and architects, seduced by nature and minimalism, moved into a XIXth century farmhouse. Antiquities and contemporary art converge in an atmosphere that is continuously renewed, at the cadence of their acquisitions. The owners of this place, being used at the same time as single family home and Polyèdre's headquarter, warmly welcome you twice a year. Restructuring spaces, as in this old 1895 fruit plantation, searching for quality materials, authentic furniture, items of curiosity, colours and fabrics and combining them in a contemporary ambience. Such is the challenge assigned to Henri-Charles and Natasha Hermans.

www.polyedre.be

Tangled up in white, the bedroom housed under the roof, is a haven of serenity. Furniture pieces and items of various styles and eras are inviting for the journey...
Bed adorned with a small oak bench, achieved at the Polyèdre work studio.

LUXURY AND LIGHTNESS

The master suite (pages 52-53) in this manor radiates luxury and lightness. The bedroom is open to the ridge with nice oak trusses. A closed gas fireplace with an oak frame creates extra warmth in this room. Lively fabrics and warm natural colours make for the finishing touch. The guestroom (above and on page 51) fully connects to the nice romantic atmosphere of the house, and has a lovely garden view.

www.costermans-projecten.be

LA SOURCE

"La Source" is a sixteenth century stately home set in the Gascogne region and whose farm buildings have recently been fully renovated by interior designer Sarah Lavoine. Everything still had to be done: recovering the old stones from the outer walls, restructuring the garden, redrawing the boundaries of the rooms, building a swimming pool, and so on, and for once Sarah Lavoine herself was the customer. As soon as she acquired this domain, Sarah Lavoine knew exactly what it was she wanted: a large family home full of friends, with many living areas and large, very comfortable rooms for everyone. Sarah Lavoine modernised her house and at the same time gave it a warmer atmosphere. It was an enormous project and there is still a lot of work to be done, but the advantage of a holiday residence is that you can take all the time you need. Each room is named after the colour of the parquet (red, green, blue, etc.).

www.sarahlavoine.com

View of several rooms, harmonised in hues of white and sage green ensuring a soft touch with the large black window frames providing the only contrast. A mixture of furniture with a mottled look and Moroccan carpets on the white parquet. The shutters of the room are made of raw pine, they move along visible rails.

↖
The master bedroom. All house linen was custom-made by "Chez Zoé". The doors of the old paneling have been stripped.

MONOCHROME WHITE

This bedroom painted in monochrome white is part of a beautiful country house in Canadian wood skeleton construction by Vincent Bruggen.

www.vincentbruggen.be

The night hall with a view of the dressing room and the bedroom.
The dressing room door with window allows access to the first bathroom.
Seats : Toy from Starck.

INSPIRED BY AMSTERDAM

Originally Annemarie and Robert wanted renovation plans designed for their house in the green environment of Antwerp. However, Paul Vanrunxt, from the building company Vincent Bruggen, instead suggested to knock down the existing house and to build a house inspired by the Amsterdam canal-side houses. To his own surprise they immediately agreed with this proposition. Annemarie and Robert came to Paul Vanrunxt after a visit in his show-house in Keerbergen. The clients immediately knew that they wanted to cooperate with Vincent Bruggen. It seemed that the company was specialized in Canadian wood skeleton construction. The owners weren't directly looking for that, but upon hearing more about the principles and advantages of this construction style they were immediately hooked.

www.vincentbruggen.be

For the dressing room the owner has chosen a high polished white.

CONTEMPORARY CLASSIC

Christel De Vos has designed this bedroom with furniture from RR Interior
Concepts: modern design and objects with a warm, timeless aura.

www.devos-interieur.be

A PENTHOUSE APARTMENT IN THE DOCKLANDS

CarterTyberghein were asked to design the interior of the penthouse apartment on the 18th floor of a building situated in the Docklands with dramatic views along the Thames. They were given the dimensions and produced schematic layouts to turn the penthouse into a three-bedroom luxury apartment with a grand entrance area leading onto a spacious terrace. To echo the shape of the building, they introduced a curved entrance hall to the heart of the apartment. From this space, rooms lead off through full-height custom-designed dark-stained Indian rosewood doors, which enhance the height of the rooms. The contrast of dark timber and light finishes is sustained throughout the apartment. As so much of the apartment is glazed, it was possible to create drama with the darker finishes, whilst still retaining a sense of airiness.

www.cartertyberghein.com

A view of the guest bedroom showing the crackle finish on the wardrobe doors with their bronze handles. Armoire designed for the client.

↖
The silk panelled wall behind the bed gives a tailored and luxurious look to the bedroom. Wall lights maximise the space on the custom-designed bedside tables.

A MAJESTIC COUNTRY ESTATE

This country estate, situated on the outskirts of Sint-Genesius-Rode and Waterloo, is surrounded by a magnificent garden of several hectares, every corner of which has a different atmosphere. Esther Gutmer completely redesigned the space, which was classic in style and not well-suited to modern needs, ensuring that the four members of this family could experience comfort, elegance, light and functionality throughout the whole house.

www.esthergutmer.be

The guestroom.

↖
An armchair and accessories
by Ralph Lauren in this
bedroom.

SHADES OF WHITE

This house "with its feet in the water" in the parkland of Saint-Tropez boasts magnificent views, but had been neglected for many years. Esther Gutmer created a completely new structure, dividing the house into three living spaces, with all rooms enjoying a sea view. The outside areas and the garden were redesigned and offer a splendid 180° panorama. The absence of a parapet ensures an uninterrupted vista. Shades of white, with just a few colourful accents as contrast, were selected for the interior, underlining the character of this haven of beauty.

www.esthergutmer.be

A view from the bathroom, which is separated from the bedroom by white wooden shutters.

↖
The master bedroom opens
out onto the teakwood
gangway.

REDIVISING THE INTERNAL SPACE

Esther Gutmer completely renovated this duplex apartment in a three-storey building in the centre of Brussels dating from 1921.
The distinctive character of this home, with its perfectly symmetrical semi-hexagonal shape, lies in the way all of the rooms open to the front of the building.
The huge windows allow plenty of light to fill the apartment.
Esther Gutmer has redivided the internal space, and also redesigned all of the details of the walls, the floors, the ceilings and the woodwork.

www.esthergutmer.be

↖
The unit and headboard are
in high gloss Macassar ebony.
Walls are upholstered in
squares made of suede.
Ralph Lauren bedside tables.

A SERENE ATMOSPHERE

A classical residence underwent a thorough metamorphosis,
spurred on by Nathalie Van Reeth.
The house was fully stripped, down to the basic structure.
The rear was torn open to strengthen the contact with the sunny
garden and improve the incidence of light. Materials and colour
were added subtly to accentuate the serene atmosphere.

nathalie.vanreeth@skynet.be

The dressing was custom made according to a design by Nathalie Van Reeth. Cupboards in high-shine varnish with a tinted oak veneer finish for the interior.

Colour continuity in the bedroom, but designed in different materials. Night side tables India Mahdavi, sheets by Mia Zia. The serene, intimate atmosphere remains omnipresent.

CHEZ ODETTE

As a tribute to the owner of a small bistro in the village, the property developer named her new hotel "Chez Odette", a charming guesthouse with six rooms and a refined kitchen. The new hotel proved to be very much to the taste of many city dwellers who visited the village and the decision was taken to design an annex on the other side of the square… Two rooms, a suite and a conference room, a bar and a sitting room, all designed by Ensemble & Associés in close cooperation with the property developer.

www.ensembleetassocies.be

The suite in the annex.

ODETTE EN VILLE

"Chez Odette" is the ideal base for city residents to explore the remote Gaume region. Today there is also "Odette en ville", to re-experience this success story in Brussels as well.
A place like no other in the capital, truly worthy of a metropolis.
Eight rooms that respect the distinctive whole of this resident to the tiniest detail, with a harmonious mix of original mouldings, natural materials and details from yesteryear.

www.ensembleetassocies.be

The dressing was custom-made with brush painted medium and grey tinted glass.

↖
A desk designed by Ensemble & Associés and finished in glossy chrome and a mirror surface in grey-tinted glass. A chair by Marcel Wanders.

SOBER COLOURS, PERFECT LIGHTING

Sober colours, perfect lighting, a warm feeling: an exclusive
bedroom, designed by Brigitte Garnier.

www.garnier.be

HARMONY OF WHITE IN AN ANCIENT CASTLE

It took two years for the efforts of Hendrik Vermoortel and Ingrid Lesage to transform Kasteel Ter Heyde in Vladslo (Diksmuide), supposedly founded on a castle-mound structure with origins in the fourteenth century, into a contemporary castle home. Over the course of time, it is intended that this protected monument should develop into a cultural enclave: a meeting place where the arts, as well as philosophy, sociology, architecture and the preservation of historic buildings, can enter into constant interaction.

www.buro2.be

Elements of the old beam construction can still be seen in the completely white bedroom. A bed by Starck.

↖
The master bedroom has been accommodated in the original owl tower with the Gothic windows: the openings in the walls, which are several metres high, create sublime light effects.

CLASSIC CONTEMPORARY
IN A VILLA INSPIRED BY NORMANDY

This villa, typical of Normandy, has been renovated by architect Christine
von der Becke and interior designer Nathalie Van Reeth.
The idea was to retain the charm and style of the original
house: not extreme, minimal architecture,
but interior spaces that have in part been adapted to contemporary
needs. The result shows an open and restful unity.

nathalie.vanreeth@skynet.be   www.christinevonderbecke.be

The dressing room, created by Nathalie Van Reeth, is also in lacquered MDF and walnut. The top of the central piece of furniture has been covered in white leather. The light was made to order.

↖
The furniture in the parents'
bedroom was custom-made
in white lacquered MDF and
walnut.

EPISCOPAL INSPIRATION

This residence for a family with three growing children was built by
architect Bernard De Clerck in a classic eighteenth-century style:
he drew his inspiration from a bishop's country seat near Bruges, which dates back to 1750.
The quality of the light, the creation of perspectives and the optimal
orientation of the rooms were important in the design of this house.
All the spaces are arranged around an inner courtyard, which means that the
occupants can enjoy the sunlight in different rooms for most of the day.

info@bernarddeclerck.be

The daughter's bedroom is finished in pale shades.

The son's bedroom in browner shades.

↖
The large bedroom with its oak ceiling and floor. A 'chaise brisée'.

RENOVATION OF A HISTORIC FINCA

La Carrascosa, a historic finca near Jerez de la Frontera (southern Spain), is situated on the foothills of a wild and untouched scenic area that stretches for around eighty kilometres along the Bay of Cadiz, almost as far as the rock of Gibraltar. The owner, a well-travelled businessman, wanted to create a property that would be easy to use in the warm summer months as well as the sometimes unpredictable winter period, for board meetings as well as for holidays and hunting.

www.christinebekaert.be

Four of the six pairs of eighteenth-century shutters slide away behind the leather walls.
The headboard is designed to mirror the fireplace wall with its spacious built-in cupboards made from ayous planks. The bronze lanterns have a hidden electric light in the top. The oak floor has been given a tropical-wood patina.

↖
Belgian linen has been used for the headboard and the canopy, which is suspended from heavy, hand-forged chains. The sofa is covered with a kilim that was found in Turkey. The Ceutericks found the old leather saddle, embroidered with golden thread (on the wall to the left) in the souks of Fez, and the lanterns in Marrakech.

The headboard is made from old cedar-wood doors with their naturally acquired patina.
The window shutters have been given a matching patina by Kordekor. A subtle limewash finish strengthens the relaxed, close-to-nature feeling.

ANNO 1642

This house, dating back to 1642, with its four bays and saddleback roof in the traditional brick and sandstone style and its abutting nineteenth-century buildings, has been restored and radically re-modelled by architect Bernard De Clerck to make it a fully fledged contemporary home for a family with three young children. The owners wished to put all the rooms to their best use, enjoying the magnificent surroundings and making use of the natural light, orientation and straightforward materials such as stone, wood and whitewash.

info@bernarddeclerck.be

The old beams in the parents' bedroom have been restored and left unfinished. The oak walls divide the room up and create a dressing space. Whitewashed walls brighten up the colour palette.

THE COMPLETE TRANSFORMATION
OF A BELLE EPOQUE COUNTRY HOUSE

This Belle Epoque country house was built in three phases.
The original house was a modestly proportioned hunting lodge dating from 1890.
Two more sections were added in 1904 and 1920.
The house has recently undergone a painstaking process of
restoration, under the enthusiastic direction of the owner.
She has renovated the historic country house in a 'gentle' way, full of
respect for the authentic architectural elements of the property.

The parents' dressing room, with its ceiling-height painted wardrobes in the background.

↖
The master bedroom.

FRESHENING UP
A RESTORED FARMHOUSE

This 19th-century farmhouse with a courtyard has been
freshened up and given a more contemporary feel.
Original elements were retained as far as possible, and nothing
about the existing structure of the house was changed: a gentle renovation.

The existing wooden floor was bleached. A Vi-Spring bed and a sofa by Flamant.

The dressing room beside the parents' bedroom, with ceiling-height cupboards in bleached oak. Modular spotlights.

TIMELESS, MINIMALIST INTERIOR

A London art collector asked Mark Mertens (am projects) to refurbish her residence and provide for the interior decoration. The aim was to design a timeless, minimalist interior in which the art collection would be set off to best effect. For this reason the decision was taken to maintain the existing original elements of the residence, and restore these where necessary.

www.amprojects.be

Bed, headboard and door hardware from the am projects "Actuals" collection. The cupboards were made in MDF and painted along with the walls.

PEACE AND QUIET

This renovation project in the green environs around Antwerp was entrusted to Sphere Concepts. They contacted architect Gerd Van Zundert (AID-Architects) to adapt the outer walls and to bring these into the correct proportions, after Sphere Concepts had designed the interior layout. The previous layout of the villa was dated, and Sphere Concepts replaced this with an interior that radiates charm, and in particular peace and quiet.

www.sphereconcepts.be

The dressing unit with seam in patchwork cow skin, like the headboard at the end of the bed. A carpet under the bed in longhaired tufted linen and wool (Limited Edition).

THE BEDROOMS OF A LAKESIDE RESIDENCE

This summer house on Lake Geneva used to be part of the «Domaine de Chanivaz». It was bought by a young family and fully renovated by Sphere Concepts. Located on a spit of land between Geneva and Laussane in the Vaud, this estate has a fabulous view over the French side of Lake Leman where you can admire the snow-capped mountains even in summer. The listed outer walls were conserved, but inside the residence all dividing walls and mezzanine floors were taken out, and raised where possible. The residence was given a completely new floor plan and fitted out with an extra room as a guest accommodation unit built into the mountain. The microclimate means that living in «Les Fontanettes» is simply marvellous.

www.sphereconcepts.be

Lampshades flank the bed instead of the traditional small lampshades.
A Nilson bed with custom-made headboard in bed linen from Society and Gwendolino.

The master suite has a separate dressing room.

ANGLO-SAXON INSPIRATION

Ilse De Meulemeester created this residence in close cooperation with villa builder
Elbeko and the architects' firm of engineer and architect Bart François.
The assignment seemed simple: to design a timeless country house with the historical impact
of a traditional English cottage, which would be a beacon of peace and quiet and a place
with a permanent holiday feel to it. The main building draws on Anglo-Saxon inspiration.

www.ilsedemeulemeester.be   wwww.bartfrancois.be

The master bedroom, with its padded headboard, high skirting boards, and wide-plank parquet floor, is redolent with the grandeur of a grand hotel. The bed linen is embroidered with the initials "IDM". Curtains in heavy taffeta, finished off at the top with loops. The radiator cupboards have a duckboard grille.

A DESIGNER'S HOME IN CAPE TOWN

Project architects Richard Townsend and Stefan Antoni used a 'sea-farm' inspiration
to create a holiday house for a small family in Cape Town (South Africa).
The house was to have a feature double volume space with very simple clean
lines and needed to flow seamlessly between interior and exterior.
The clients, being in the design world, were particularly sensitive to colour and were very
much involved in choosing the materials used in both the interior and exterior of the home.

www.saota.com

The guest bedroom looks out over the bay with a private terrace and balau timber pergola.

↖
The master bedroom is an experience in subtle luxury,
with a rabbit fur throw draped over an ottoman at the
foot of the bed. David Reade glass bedside lamps rest on
washed oak bedside tables, and a delicate mother of pearl
curtain hangs against the feature wall.   The headboard
and matching bed base are both of fine Indian cotton.

A LUXURIOUS MIXTURE

This mountain chalet is set amidst picturesque scenery in the French Alps. The traditional architecture was reinterpreted so that the magnificent views could be enjoyed to best effect, whilst the interior is a luxurious mixture of style, comfort and a modern lifestyle. The design team of Moulder, Laxer + Salter of F3 Architects in London worked together with Base Contracts and local professionals in order to complete this extraordinary residence and have it ready for immediate occupation.

www.f3architects.co.uk   www.basecontracts.com

The little tables at the foot of
the bed are by Robert Kuo.

THE BEDROOMS OF CHALET CHASSEFORÊT

Interior architect Marie-France Stadsbader designed the interior of this
chalet Chasseforêt, located on the ski runs of Courchevel.
Descamps was responsible for the custom-made items in this chalet.

mst@cantillana.com   www.descamps.be

ROUGEMONT CHALET

This chalet in the village of Rougemont (Pays d'Enhaut, Switzerland) was designed
by the Rougemont-based firm of interior architects Tamara's
Design (Federica and Tamara Sessa).

www.tamarasdesign.com

The wall covering is edged with a wooden frame.

The guest room with white roughcast walls and wooden framing is bathed in a linen mastic atmosphere.

↖
The bed and curtains are dressed with dark-chestnut coloured flannel edged in natural linen. The photograph is by André Brito.

A LOFT WITH A BREATHTAKING VIEW OF THE CAPITAL

This loft, situated on the top floor of a converted industrial building, has been completely reorganised by interior architect Anne Derasse.
All of the functions flow together in the same space. The master bedroom with bathroom and dressing room is alongside a large central rectangle.

www.annederasse.be

The guestroom is in shades of brick and chocolate. Headboard and carpet in woven leather. Silk curtains and bedspread in ribbed velvet.

The second guestroom is a harmony of slate-grey and purple. Curtains in satinised cotton and a bedspread in damask with a geometric design.

↖
The foot of the bed in the master bedroom was designed by Anne Derasse; the flat-screen TV is integrated into this unit. The wooden lid opens automatically when the TV lift mechanism is activated. To the left and right of the bed, symmetrical entrances to the bathroom and dressing room. Silk curtains, floor in solid wengé.

A MASTER BEDROOM IN PURE WHITE

This master bedroom in a project by Olivier Michel (architect Bruno Corbisier) is pure white, except for the art by Charles Szymkowicz. The carpet by Limited Edition creates a cosy atmosphere. An ipé bed with a velvet finish and night lights by Melograno.

EIGHTEENTH-CENTURY INSPIRATION
FOR A COUNTRY MANOR

Architect Bernard De Clerck designed a country manor in a traditional style for a young family that enjoys an informal way of life and being in close contact with nature: quiet, calming and sophisticated. The eighteenth century was an important source of inspiration for this project. Bernard De Clerck created the whole house: outside as well as inside. His clients gave him a great deal of support with this, as did the capable specialists who carried out his designs to the smallest detail. For some rooms (the bathrooms and the bedrooms for the children and guests), he called upon the expertise of interior designer Christine Bekaert.

info@bernarddeclerck.be   www.christinebekaert.be

The daughter's bedroom makes a calm impression, with its bleached oak floor and simple four-poster bed in light fabrics.

The master dressing rooms were finished in oak and painted.

↖
A guest room and a
bathroom for children.
The partition wall is made
of old pine planks.

Louis XVI panelling
has been adapted to fit
the master bedroom.
Above the bed there is a
contemporary work by
Jean-Marc Louis.

A NEW LIFE

A country house located at the border of two Southern Tuscany valleys (Val d'Orcia and Valdichiana) and abandoned for many years, was discovered by its present owner in the late 90's. With the support of interior decorator Paola Navone and landscape architect Peter Curzon and with a lot of love and patience, he transformed it into his permanent residence. Formerly a fashion industry executive, he now enjoys his new farmer's life, producing wine and olive oil.

Two of the guest suites. Each has the walls painted in a different color and is named after that color. All the suites have separate sitting rooms and bathrooms.

RESPECTFUL RESTORATION OF A FARMHOUSE
FROM 1689

The entrance is adorned with the historic farmhouse's year of construction: 1689.
However, some parts of the house date back to the fifteenth century, and it is also suspected
that the farmhouse used to be a stopping point for monks
travelling from Florence to Vallombrosa.
The current owners started restoring the farmhouse at the end of 1997.
The work, directed by architect Claudio Calcinai and antiquarian/
interior specialist Axel Vervoordt, took a year and a half.

All the bedrooms were decorated by Axel Vervoordt with subtle colour schemes to create a serene, rural atmosphere. The original features were retained wherever possible, but contemporary comfort has been introduced.

A REFUGE IN HOLLAND PARK

This stately residence in London's Holland Park was built in 1862 by the architects William & Francis Radford. Winny Vangroenweghe, architect with Obumex, created and coordinated the complete renovation and layout of the premises into a timeless and harmonious whole, where the hectic character of the metropolis is quickly forgotten… Obumex has over half a century's experience in the design and production of exclusive, customised interiors.

www.obumex.be

The dressing room designed by Obumex also emanates refinement and calm.

FULLY COSTUMISED

Pascal van der Kelen has been one of the leading architects and interior designers of his generation for several years. As well as his own customised architecture and interior designs, he has also recently unveiled his own Home Collection. This apartment shows how Pascal van der Kelen combines bespoke work, made using the architect's drawings, with elements from his Home Collection.

www.pascalvanderkelen.com

The parents' dressing room is situated between the bedroom and the bathroom and is fully customised from drawings by the architect. On the left the fronts are made from lacquer ware, on the right in grey smoked glass.

↖
The parents' bedroom. Bed and headboard from the Home Collection by Pascal van der Kelen. The bed is made here from bog oak in combination with white flannel for the headboard, and bedside cabinets painted in off-white gloss.

A COMPLETE REDESIGN

Interior architect Sarah Lavoine was given a carte blanche for this complete project in the heart of Paris: the transformation of a duplex apartment with 250 m² + 200 m² terraces. The renovation works took a long time because the original kitchen and entrance hall were situated on the upper floor. Sarah Lavoine designed these rooms below, so the eighth floor could be devoted completely to the master bedroom with desk, dressing room, bathroom and wet room. The whole thing was completely redesigned by Sarah Lavoine's team: creation of the spaces, customisation, the succession of volumes...

www.sarahlavoine.com

The master bedroom is central in the open area on the upper floor to increase the feeling of space and make circulation around it possible.
The desk behind it also serves as a headboard.
Dressing room in a combination of grey and black-coloured oak with a low bespoke cupboard for storing shirts.
There is a very comfortable fitted carpet in natural linen.
The large mirror reflects the terraces. Hanging lamps designed by Sarah Lavoine. The bed linen and the cover are from Sarah Lavoine's decoration company "Chez Zoé".

PEACE AND QUIET

The design of this low energy home, created by the architect Annik Dierckx, is timeless and practical. The newest materials and most recent technologies were used. The master bedroom, with its own dressing room and bathroom, forms the private space for the parents and can be closed off completely. The custom-made built-in storage wall along the entire length of the corridor offers a lot of storage space: essential in this home.

annik.dierckx@telenet.be

A WARM TOUCH

As one of the few modern homes in the surrounding, the atmosphere of the
contemporary architecture continues indoors: large and high rooms with a
lot of light, and the use of sober materials in a tight framework.
Obumex's design still results in an interior with a warm touch, the natural
materials, the shades of grey outside and white inside, the balanced
colour packages, with here and there a contemporary accent.
This is a project that is fully designed, implemented and co-ordinated by Obumex.

www.obumex.be

A TIMELESS AND LUXURIOUS UNIVERSE

Interior Architects Brigitte Boiron and John-Paul Welton continue their cooperation
further and provide the complete renovation of this apartment of 320 m²
located in a historic building in Geneva. They created a timeless and luxurious
universe that will honour their art collection, a wish of the residents.
The company Project Design was responsible for the complete renewal of the rooms.
Under the leadership of Brigitte Boiron the decoration became a perfect blend of the many
works of art and the custom-made furniture. John-Paul Welton shows his expertise: the
creation and implementation of a part of the furniture, autographed by Welton Design.

www.projectdesign.ch   www.weltondesign.com

The master bedroom. A bed, a bedside table on a chromium-plated base and a sofa by Welton Design. Decortex Briosa curtains and a parquet floor in tinted oak. Farrow & Ball paints. A pouf by Promemoria.

TRANSPARENCY, LIGHTNESS AND LUMINOSITY

Located on top of a promontory, this villa was completely restructured "feet in the water» style, and enlarged by GEF Réalisations, the office for interior design. Transparency, lightness and luminosity were the keywords in this project. The interior design, which is extended outdoors and in the garden, was subtly designed by landscape designer Loup & Co., who extends the architectural reflex to the sea.

www.loupandco.com

The master suite with a large private terrace. The effect of this space (with dressing room, bedroom and bathroom) shows the ingenuity of the architects, who perfectly combine lightness and transparency.

A REAL ICON

An architect-designed bungalow from 1959 was spectacularly transformed
into an icon of contemporary minimalist aesthetics and exclusive modern-
day living comfort by Van Aken Architects of Eindhoven.
Zeth Interior design & construction (interior designer Rob Zeelen)
was responsible for the design of this unique home.

www.vanakenarchitecten.nl   www.zeth.nl

A bed by Schramm Gala, seating by Porro Truffle.

This bed is by Ivano Redaelli (model B). The pouf and chaise longue are also by Redaelli.

COSMOPOLITAN FEELING

This complete structure was designed by interior architect
Nathalie Deboel in collaboration with Obumex.
In consultation with the client Obumex chose for the ground floor: a fully customised
and personalised interior, where the client can find complete peace and harmony.
The consistent use of dark tinted Spanish oak and bronze gives the interior a warm
atmosphere. This allows the contemporary artworks to come perfectly into their own.
The combination of a timeless and elegant interior with art
and antique results in a cosmopolitan whole.

www.obumex.be   www.nathaliedeboel.be

The floors were made by the firm Vendredi. At the client's request an intimate atmosphere was created by the use of dark tones and hand-cut mosaic. A custom-made carpet (Peter Bross) in the same tints as the cabinets in high gloss lacquer.

The children's bedroom with chairs by Poul Kjaerholm. The striped wall was inspired by the work of Daniel Buren.

↖
The old roof structure was restored. In combination with the contemporary design this results in a suite feeling.

A LOFT IN AMSTERDAM

Despite the fact that this house was handed over completely new,
the basic structure still had to be adapted completely.
Rob Zeelen of Zeth Interior architecture & implementation, together with Lucien van
de Ven of B-Dutch and Jos van Zijl (Jos van Zijl Design) designed the space.
The client wanted a sober, functional and timeless interior,
in which the designers succeeded admirably.

www.zeth.nl

A sliding door by Rimadesio Graphis and a Rimadesio Zenit closet.

↖
A bed by Schramm Gala
and wall Lamps by Modular
Nomad Minimal Shade.
Bedside tables Brute Design.

A HOUSE IN THE LUXEMBOURG COUNTRYSIDE

This house was built in 2007 and is situated in the Luxembourg countryside. The interior combines both neutral and timeless elements with some antiques, using natural and noble materials. The house is also used as a show-room for the owners' interior design and decoration business: In Tempo by Luc Leroi. Their philosophy lies in the creation of timeless interiors favouring materials such as natural wood, stone, lime, linen and an overarching use of artisanal work.

www.intempo.lu

The master bedroom has been rendered in white lime-wash paint. An Anker bedding bed
with Libeco linen cover. Wall-lights from Galerie des lampes – Paris.

↖
This floor is set aside as
guest suite. A pine wardrobe
originally from the Pyrenees.

A WEEKEND HOUSE IN THE HASPENGOUW AREA

This property is located in Haspengouw, a few kilometres from Tongres, and is used as a second home. The interior is characterised by an exceptional inflow of light afforded by the double exposure from the row of main rooms in succession. The spirit of Normandy houses can be found in the design from In Tempo by Luc Leroi.

www.intempo.lu

AN OASIS OF CALM AND SIMPLICITY

An old presbytery from 1765 had become completely neglected by the end of the 1990s. This historic house has been restored in an authentic way. Interior architect Nathalie Van Reeth has created a timeless whole that does hot harm the historic character of the existing house.

nathalie.vanreeth@yucom.be

The bedroom is an oasis of calm and simplicity. The light-grey and white shades give this room a serene atmosphere. The sleeping area and the dressing room flow into each other.
MDF furniture with leather handles. The new pinewood floor has been given a dark tint. The fireplace has been restored to its original condition and simply plastered.

HARMONY OF BLACK AND WHITE

Following a successful career in business, Alexander Cambron now creates around three completely ready-to-use, top-quality residential projects a year, in both contemporary and timelessly classic designs. These are "pret-à-habiter" homes for top executives and their families, with the focus entirely on the wishes and requirements of the new owners.

www.alexandershouses.com   www.fabathome.be

The master bedroom in black and white with an open fireplace connecting the dressing room and bedroom. All of the rooms have a view of the back garden.

The black dressing room of the master suite is in oak veneer, with a see-through gas fire.

THE ART OF LIVING ON THE CÔTE D'AZUR

In this project Christel De Vos concentrated entirely on the complete furnishing and finishing. Both for outside and inside the furniture selected came from Flexform, B&B Italia, Minotti, Maxalto,… The object was to create a pleasant environment where the surroundings and the finished interior form a single united whole. Fresh colours, in combination with a black contrast, show a controlled vision.

www.devos-interieur.be

A THREE BEDROOM APARTMENT

This model apartment at the seaside was created by RR Interior Concepts.
The apartment contains a master bedroom with a dressing
room, a second bedroom and a smaller one.

www.rrinterieur.be

STREAMLINED, CLASSIC AND CHIC

Chris van Eldik and Wendy Jansen opened an interior-design company about ten years ago in Wijk bij Duurstede in the Netherlands, called De Zon van Duurstede (The Sun of Duurstede). Their style can best be described as "streamlined classic": a combination of warm, natural, honest, basic materials and fabrics, but in a definitely contemporary, almost minimalist setting. This husband-and-wife team were among the pioneers of lime paints, which have enjoyed great success in recent years. The choice of these paints is completely in keeping with their designs, which are timeless, sober and cosy, all at the same time.

www.jobinterieur.nl

A Nilson bed with custom-made padded headboard in white linen. The floor has a white painted finish. Bed linen by Society, blind in grey Egyptian cotton.

Max armchair with footstool. A tall, white-painted linen cupboard.

A GENTLE TRANSFORMATION

Interior architect Francis Luypaert was commissioned to renovate
this home and to transform it in a sympathetic way.

www.francisluypaert.be

The warm, natural shades in the bedroom suite create a cosy, homely atmosphere. The built-in and indirect lighting accentuates the features of the room. All of the furniture was designed to complement this space. The niches have the same finish as the walls.

The existing floor was treated to give it a paler finish, then coated with a semi-matte varnish.

The furniture is in vertical Oregon veneer, with a brushed, tinted and matte varnished finish. Blinds in linen and standing lamps in brushed chrome.

The bathroom is also in Oregon veneer. The surface is in Moleanos natural stone. LED lighting was chosen for the niche behind the bath.

SOPHISTICATED SIMPLICITY IN A DISTINCTIVE COUNTRY HOME

Husband-and-wife team Alain and Brigitte Garnier fitted out this attractive country
house in a timeless style that is casual and sophisticated at the same time.
Verraes Decoratie carried out the painting work.

www.garnier.be

A chaise longue with white linen covers. An eighteenth-century Italian trestle table with a walnut-wood armchair.
Bedspread by Chelsea Textiles and all curtains by C&C, fabric and production by Garnier.

LIVING AND WORKING IN PERFECT HARMONY

Architect Lie Ulenaers faced an important challenge when designing her own home and work space. She had to combine a very compact private residence with an office on the first floor. The total design, furnishing and detailing result in an optimal division of both zones, which are still perfectly in harmony in a timeless atmosphere. The consistently thorough white/black highlights reinforce the spatial effect. White gives continuous nuances according to the incidence of the light. As a neutral background this colour also constantly contrasts with the people and objects in the interior. The limited materials and choice of colours ensure calm and coherence in all living spaces. The home was constructed in perfect consultation by the company Vincent Bruggen.

www.architectulenaers.be

You can reach the dressing room from the bathroom. The dressing rooms were custom designed by Lieke Ulenaers and realised by Vincent Bruggen. The sober black/white line is consistently continued here.

A CONTEMPORARY APARTMENT IN GSTAAD

Tamara's Design was commissioned to design a weekend getaway home in Gstaad (in the Swiss Alps). The owners wanted anything but an Alpine interior: the arrangement of the internal spaces and the decoration are purposely very austere and modern for this apartment that the owners occupy mainly at weekends. The serene atmosphere in this apartment is enhanced by the sense of unity in the choice of materials and colour schemes: the doors, the cabinets and the parquet flooring made of dark stained oak contrast with the monastic white of the walls. Spaciousness was also an important aspect underpinning the creation of this interior.

www.tamarasdesign.com

This child's bedroom features square leather wall panels and night tables by Tamara's Design.

This boy's bedroom is awash with black/grey hues. Curtains with a black/grey flannel check motif by Andrew Martin.

↖
In the master bedroom, the walls are covered with white leather panels framed by a dark stained oak structure. The night tables (also made of dark stained oak) are the creation of Tamara's Design.
The white curtains and the Japanese screen in voile and leather by Elitis enhance the Zen atmosphere of this bedroom.

SOBER AND SERENE

In this report, interior architect Alexis Herbosch presents a renovation project in Wilrijk.
The main bedroom/bathroom/dressing-room area of this house was designed in a muted
harmony of white and écru, combined with a touch of dark brown in the bedroom.
By demolishing a wall, Alexis Herbosch created a connection between two separate rooms.
Pivoting doors close off the rooms and create different atmospheres.

www.herbosch-vanreeth.be

A white-painted walk-in dressing room in this chocolate-brown room, creating a strong contrast.

White wardrobes in the dressing room with open shelves in the centre.

↖
The master bedroom is a
white room with accents
in dark stained oak. The
existing fireplace was
retained.
Bed in chocolate brown.

AN *EN SUITE* BEDROOM

A master bedroom with dressing room designed by Annick Grimmelprez. High
folding doors in walnut separate the two rooms. A solid oak floor.
Dressing room furniture in solid oak and solid walnut shutters.

info@annickgrimmelprez.be

AN OASIS OF CALM ON THE BELGIAN COAST

This apartment on the Belgian coast was designed by interior architect Philip Simoen and built by Guido Dedeyne construction company. They aimed to make consistent use of two materials throughout the apartment: bleached teakwood and Belgian bluestone. This harmonious look is suffused with an atmosphere of peace and serenity.

www.simoeninterieur.be

A REMARKABLE RESTORATION

Chris van Eldik and Wendy Jansen, owners of JOB Interiors, carefully restored a 16th-century building into a contemporary living space.

www.jobinterieur.nl

ENDLESS VIEWS

Nothing remains of the original appearance of these four houses from the 1950s which were combined into a contemporary and luxurious single-family home. The restructuring of its various levels and functionality revolved around a patio which now lets natural light into the heart of the house. With taste and determination, the owner allowed Oliver and Hélène Lempereur to go to the end with their ideas.

www.olivierlempereur.com

FAMILY LIFE

Unconditional supporters of the Lempereurs' work, the owners trusted them from beginning to end. They also followed their advice for the design of an area entirely dedicated to their three children, in order to keep another one reserved for the parents. They agreed to the wonderful idea of designing the bathroom as an opening onto the Milky Way.

www.olivierlempereur.com

A TRIBUTE TO CONTEMPORARY ART

In this collector's apartment, art played a central role in the space planning that Hélène and Olivier Lempereur elaborated. Inspiration, information and physical spaces are the ultimate key to complete the final look of the interior, art work have guided the story of the project from the beginning. For the Lempereur, heritage of work of art often determines the design of spaces: the nature and proportion of a wall, the location of a door, the light sources, and the arrangement of a room.

www.olivierlempereur.com

CHIC AND COSMOPOLITAN

This is an apartment that is lived in, where people entertain, where children play and grow up. The amicable relationship that grew after a meeting with the owners enabled a subtle translation of the "couture" style embodied by the head of the household. The old parquet floor was kept as were some mouldings. On the other hand, the ceilings were reworked in keeping with the cornices in order to place mechanical elements and lighting. The noblesse of the materials and the refinement of the finishing give this apartment a universal style. Its atmosphere is thoroughly cosmopolitan.

www.olivierlempereur.com

AN OASIS OF CALM IN THE CENTRE OF THE CITY

Maison Delaneau is a small boutique hotel with an Urban Spa, located in the centre of Antwerp, in the heart of the fashion and art district in the South. Maison Delaneau has ten exclusive en suite rooms, a few of which include a jacuzzi, open fireplace, private garden or sauna. The layout is sleek, timeless and design oriented, in perfect harmony with the natural materials and advanced technology. The elegant architecture stands for Japanese philosophy: serene, plain, pure and aesthetic. Harmoniously balanced treatment rooms and experienced therapists ensure a unique experience of beauty and holistic healing, a blend of ancient mystical recipes and a contemporary approach. Delaneau Spa is a unique experience and the ultimate indulgence: an oasis of calm and relaxation in the centre of busy city life.

www.maisondelaneau.com

A few en suite rooms at Maison Delaneau have a gas fireplace.

TIMELESS LUXURY

In this report, Alexander Cambron (Alexander's Houses) shows
the bedrooms in two of his recent residential projects.

www.alexandershouses.com

VERTICAL WALK

The garden that separates the main part of the house is south facing, the bottom of the plot presents a level area that ends 6 metres higher up. These are the only constraints to guide the architect Bruno Erpicum, who designed a residence based on two rings: a vertical ring ensures the connection between the levels, a horizontal ring includes the earth pressure at the rear and forms the interface between the main part and the rooms on the first floor. Everything is designed so as not to have to reveal the intimacy of the premises to passers-by, in this way, only a small section of the South facing garden is reserved to welcoming visitors and the entrance to the garage.

www.alexandershouses.com   www.erpicum.org

FASCINATING BLEND OF TRADITION AND MODERNITY

Where once a neglected vegetable patch grew rampant, architect
Gilles Pellerin has created an exceptional living space
in which traditional Mediterranean architecture is blended
harmoniously with contemporary elements.
The location is unique: situated on a rock halfway up a hill, with the bay of Cannes
as the décor and breathtaking views all the way from Saint-Tropez to Italy.

www.collection-privee.com

The bedroom was also finished with antique floorboards.

A guest room.

OLD AND NEW

Jan Smits and Kathy Alliët, managers of the interior design store Pas-Partoe, show in this project how old and new can be perfect partners. The new building serves as showroom, while the old rectory serves as the family home and at the same time alludes to the lifestyle philosophy of Pas-Partoe. The house shows a fascinating, surprising mix of ambience, proportions, shapes and materials amidst renowned collections (Promemoria, Flexform, Knoll, Maxalto) as well as the residents' own creations. The many different facets of living are perfectly matched here.

www.pas-partoe.be

A touch of luxury with this
Promemoria single seat,
fully covered with silk.

↖
The master bedroom. A Wanda Promemoria bed stands
against a custom-built rear wall with bronze hinges. The
bedside tables are made of steel combined with ebony.
The table lamps are also in bronze.

The bench behind the wall is custom-made and finished in glossy black. The black and white photograph is by Marc Lagrange.

SPACE AND LIGHT
IN A CONTEMPORARY COUNTRY HOUSE

This stately mansion was designed by architect Philippe Mortelmans at the behest of a
family with three young children. The interior is a creation of Annick Grimmelprez.
The house is idyllically situated in Schilde, a green suburb close to Antwerp.
Each room offers a view of the protected forest area and this house is perfectly
matched to the wishes of the owners: contemporary, with a strong feeling of light and
space, where precious materials have been used and a few colourful highlights.
The result: a cosy home in an oasis of tranquillity and wellness.

info@annickgrimmelprez.be

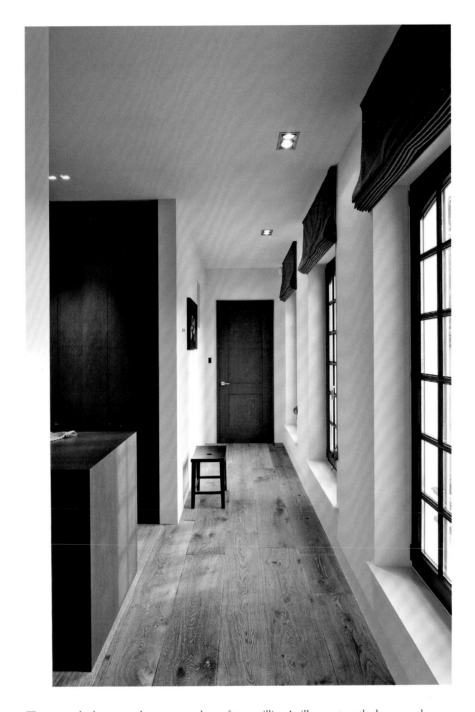

The master bedroom exudes an atmosphere of tranquillity. A silk carpet on the large wooden planks. Window frames with shutters in dark, sandblasted oak open onto a private terrace with a view on the surrounding verdant garden.

INSPIRED BY THE ENGLISH COUNTRYSIDE

Home Development Company built this English inspired villa in the green belt around Antwerp. Warm, natural materials were chosen for the exterior, perfectly in harmony with the green surroundings.

www.homedc.be

The TV was worked into a rigid wall. The air conditioning is here very subtly integrated into a line grating in the ceiling.

The fabulous master dressing was fully custom made in MDF, with a seat incorporated in the middle block.

A ZEN FEELING

This villa situated in the Kapel woodlands was renovated in close collaboration with the architect and entirely decorated by BLC Interiors. Earth tones and natural materials that create peace, space and light were used a lot: a truly Zen feeling... BLC Interiors opted for a quiet colour palette, often even ton-sur-ton. This look was extended to the upper floor.

www.blc-interiors.com

In the bedroom, the old roof trusses are still visible.
The combination of an antique mirror with an austere bed from the XVL collection and earthy tones define the atmosphere here.

A PASSION FOR BEAUTY

In this project, the architect Stéphane Boens deals in a masterly way with
the rich architectural heritage adding a very personal touch to it.
In close consultation with the owners, Boens created a unique home where tradition and artisanal
techniques, modern comfort and a passion for beauty merge into a uniquely harmonious whole.

www.stephaneboens.be   www.obumex.be

↖
The Promemoria bed features a padded headboard.
Cushions in silk.
Bedside tables: "Bomarzo" from Liaigre in bronze and
"Cassetiera" from Promemoria (lacquer and bronze).

An "Ingrid" mirror
from Promemoria and
two "St. Germain"
armchairs from Liaigre
in black metal and
leather.

LIGHT, SPACIOUS AND SUNNY

In this house Alexander Cambron, in consultation with architect Luc Toelen, has
created a true family home where light, space and a feeling of sunlight prevail.
The almost square house has large windows on all sides with views of the garden.
The interior decoration was done by Fabienne Dupont.
The attic rooms are all white and were furnished in a contemporary manner.

www.alexandershouses.com   www.fabathome.be

Floor in white painted parquet, a fireplace wall and cabinets in rough wooden panels. Furniture by Alivar.

THE LUXURY OF SPACE

Space is a luxury…
…and in this magnificent creation by Marc Corbiau, the spaces are nothing short of majestic.
Ensemble & Associés have recreated the fittings, finishes and atmosphere of
this home in order to best meet the requirements of its new owners.
Simple materials and colours, flowing lines and efficient
organisation are all hallmarks of the design.

www.ensembleetassocies.be

A PASSION FOR CONTEMPORARY ART

In a house whose lines were decided by architect Bruno Moinard (an interior designer from Paris), Obumex architect Vangroenweghe has achieved a fitting interior. The interior had to be the perfect background for the owner's artworks. So Obumex applied his proven, timeless trademarks and experience to this top project.

www.obumex.be

The dressing room of the
master bedroom with a
central block in bright pink
stained glass. Wall units and
boudoir were custom made
by Obumex. The salmon-
coloured leather seat is from
Promemoria.
Everywhere in this project
there are the specially
designed handles: double
oblique handles in a single
line.

↖
A Wanda chaise longue.

SLEEPING NATURALLY

Sleeping naturally in Nilson bedding. With a TV cabinet by
Interlübke, also from RR Interior Concepts.

www.rrinterieur.be

A custom-made walk-in wardrobe by Poliform, and a lamp by Moooi
at the foreground.
The chair in the background on the left is by Hans Wegner.
A realisation by RR Interieur in association with interior architect
Nathalie Deboel.

A Magnitude Boxspring bed.

A VISIT TO THE HOME OF A TOP INTERIOR DECORATOR IN SAINT-GERMAIN-DES-PRES

Gérard Faivre is a famous architect and interior decorator who divides his projects between his two places of residence: Provence and Paris. In Saint-Germain-des-Prés, one of the most beautiful areas of Paris, Faivre found a contemporary apartment opposite the Jardin du Luxembourg that fulfilled all of his requirements: full of light, with high ceilings, and surrounded by sufficient green to allow him to recharge, even in the French capital, after his constant trips to building sites, modern art exhibitions and trade fairs.

www.gérardfaivreparis.com

A design by Hélène and
Olivier Lempereur.

PUBLISHER
BETA-PLUS publishing
www.betaplus.com

PHOTOGRAPHY
Jo Pauwels

DESIGN
Polydem – Nathalie Binart

ISBN 13: 978-90-8944-122-5